This book
belongs to :

....

Happy Animals Coloring Book for Toddlers:
100 Funny Animals. Easy Coloring Pages For Preschool and Kindergarten.

ISBN: 9798574991794

For more informations and to stay updated on new coloring books visit our web site a
www.coloringbookkim.com

Made in United States
Troutdale, OR
11/17/2024

24925444R00058